PROTECTIVE CUSTODY

Prisoner 34042

Memorial Edition

Other Plays

By Charles LaBorde

Memorial:

A Theatrical Oral History of Americans in Vietnam

Courage:

A Drama Based on Stephen Crane's "The Red Badge of Courage"

Holocaust Duet and *Testament:*

A Two-play Variation

Affinity:

A Play of Frank Lloyd and Taliesin

All are available in paperback and as e-books on Amazon.com.

PROTECTIVE CUSTODY

Prisoner 34042

Memorial Edition

An Adaptation of the Memoir

by Dr. Susan Cernyak-Spatz

By

Charles LaBorde

PROTECTIVE CUSTODY Prisoner 34042

Copyright 2019, Revision Copyright 2021 Charles LaBorde

SPECIAL NOTE

For

Susan

The world premiere of *Protective Custody: Prisoner 34042* was produced by Three Bone Theatre, at Spirit Square's Duke Energy Theatre in Charlotte, North Carolina in November, 2019, under the direction of Dennis Delamar. Costumes were by Magda Guichard. Setting, lights, and sound design were by Ryan Maloney. Properties design was by Jackie Hohenstein. Callie Richards was stage manager. The cast was as follows:

SUSAN............. Leslie Giles
The DRESSER...Paula Baldwin

Three Bone Theatre is a professional company headed by executive director Becky Schultz and founding artistic director Robin Tynes-Miller, who also served as dramaturg for the premier production.

The first public reading of *Protective Custody: Prisoner 34042* was presented on December 13, 2018, with Nicia Carla in the role of Susan, at the second anniversary celebration of the Stan Greenspon Center for Peace and Social Justice at Queens University in Charlotte. The evening celebrated all of the Charlotte community's more than three dozen Holocaust survivors and the successes of the Greenspon Center's first two years.

This Memorial Edition has a revised ending added after Susan's death in November, 2019.

CAST OF CHARACTERS

SUSAN...A forty-something woman. She is professionally dressed and well-groomed. She is here to tell her story.

The DRESSER...A woman who assists SUSAN in costume changes. She serves at times to represent people from SUSAN's life.

SETTING

A lecture hall

A Note on the Origins of the Play

By Dennis Delamar

My friendship with Dr. Susan Cernyak-Spatz began many years ago in Charlotte, North Carolina, as members of its theatre community. We shared a love of theatre—a source of joy, entertainment, inspiration and truth for both of us. It is fitting that her inspiration and truth have guided me as director of the original production of this play about her struggle for survival. I believed in the merits of telling her inspirational story in the format of a play. It has always been the medium of communication that has meant so much to her.

The creative spark for putting Susan's story on stage came to me after directing Doug Wright's Pulitzer winning one person drama *I Am My Own Wife* in 2006. I envisioned an actress becoming Susan, while also portraying other characters in her remarkable story. Years later I shared my idea with Susan's daughter, Jackie Fishman—a friend and teaching peer. With her enthusiasm and encouragement, we contacted our favorite Charlotte playwright to run with the idea. That healthy collaboration began with our fellow educator and friend, Charles LaBorde, who brilliantly crafted this two person drama inspired by Susan's 2005 autobiography of the same name. Charles cleverly expanded my original idea to include a second character, a dresser who portrayed the other characters while assisting on stage with the many costume changes.   Our play was blessed by Susan with a few more contributions coming after the first draft was written.

Charles and I approached Robin Tynes-Miller and Becky Schultz of Three Bone Theatre to be our producers. First, there was an important reading December 13, 2018, hosted by the Stan Greenspon Center for Peace and Social Justice on the campus of Queens University in Charlotte.   Ninety-six year old Susan was able to attend and hear her story in a full house of captivated theatre-goers—a big moment for all of us.

Three Bone Theatre has provided Charles and me a nurturing environment to continue developing the piece since the reading, with further collaboration with artistic director Robin Tynes-Miller and versatile actors Leslie Giles as Susan and Paula Baldwin as the Dresser.   We are especially grateful to Magda Guichard for creating the original costumes, which are a key element in the novel staging and overall compelling uniqueness of this production.

As a director, actor, and retired public school teacher, I have a special affinity for plays that make a difference, educating and speaking to audiences about vital social issues, hopefully moving us in positive directions of change while opening our eyes to important truths and necessary conversations.

It has been an honor to collaborate with Charles on his masterpiece and to help keep Susan's vital story alive. With the current climate of anti-Semitism and with hatred and violence on the rise in our country, I have been inspired and moved by the words of my 97 year old friend: *"Never again."*

--Dennis Delamar

Director of the Original Production
of PROTECTIVE CUSTODY Prisoner 34042

PROTECTIVE CUSTODY

Prisoner 34042

An Adaptation of the Memoir

by Dr. Susan Cernyak-Spatz

By Charles LaBorde

Empty stage. Except for a rack of clothes center and a chair with a microphone on a stand near it, adjusted to the height of someone sitting in the chair.

A forty-something woman enters the stage. Adjusting her hair, appearance. Stops. Notices audience, realizes where she is and hurries down toward the audience. She hesitates as if trying to choose her words carefully. Starts to speak, then realizes she is supposed to use the microphone. Goes up to get it. Comes back down, wrestles with the cord, gets flustered, adjusts her appearance again, then refocuses on her audience.

SUSAN:

Clothes make the man. That's how the saying goes, yes? They've done a hell of a lot for this woman, too. As you can see, I have learned to "dress for success." They say that, too, don't they? Whoever "they" is—I never quite seem to know.

As you can see from the rack up there, I have a lot of clothes that have—shall we say—helped me over the years. Wait, I see some of you are checking your programs, looking around, wondering if you have wandered into the wrong lecture hall. This is not a clothing design class. No, I am supposed to tell you about my early life—a life that was interrupted and sidelined, derailed by what has come to be known as the Holocaust.

But that strikes me as too dreary a subject, even for the hour or so you are scheduled to endure me. So I have chosen to bring these clothes with me and give you a fashion show instead.

The clothes on this rack...

> *She points to it, then motions to someone in the wings. A woman, The DRESSER, enters and—when motioned to do so—moves the rack down to her. And takes the microphone from SUSAN, since it has been nothing but a bother to her.*

Thank you, dear. *(She pauses momentarily as she makes an unplanned aside.)* Before I go on, let me say this: each survivor has his own unique story. Some more harrowing, some more dramatic, some more emotional. This simply is mine. No more. No less. *(Pauses to recollect where she was.)* The clothes on this rack represent the phases in my life.

They reflect my taste, or rather, in my early years, my mother's taste in clothes appropriate for a young, I must say, somewhat affluent, Viennese girl in the 1930's.

> *DRESSER hands her the first dress. SUSAN begins to shed the professional clothes she is wearing and starts to put on the youthful dress, as she continues.*

Bear with me as I make this transition. *(As she starts to undress, she looks coyly at the audience.)* I promise to reveal only my soul tonight. I was supposed to have a screen here for modesty's sake, but apparently someone fucked up. *(She looks accusatorily at The DRESSER.)* So I will throw caution and modesty to the winds—your modesty, not mine—I lost that long ago in the camps.

> *By this time she is starting to put on the first dress.*

I was born Susannah Eckstein in Vienna in 1922. We lived in the *Silbergasse* in Dobling, then and now the best neighborhood of the city. It was an area of large vineyards and today one populated by sumptuous villas. My early years were largely uneventful and no different possibly than your own. My father was a dashing Polish lieutenant from the Great War—what you now refer to as World War I—and my mother was from an Austrian upper-middle-class family. *(Realizing she cannot fit into the childhood school dress, she holds it in front of her.)* About the time I entered first grade in the fall of 1928, they moved to Berlin to run the greeting card company they owned with one of Mother's sisters. That left me behind to start school in Vienna while living with my grandparents. Not to anyone's surprise, I am sure, they spoiled me shamelessly. Easily the best year of my young life.

Then as I started my second year of school, I found myself moved to Berlin in 1929 *(She now holds up her German school clothes.)* to be with my parents, and childhood settled into a predictable and very ordinary routine. Take your own, move it to Berlin, fill in the blanks and you have mine. Enough said.

That is true up to a point. I don't know about your parents' marriage, but I became aware early on that as running their business became difficult, routine and all-consuming, love between my parents became difficult and routine as well— anything but all-consuming. Their marriage was "interesting," with both Father and Mother finding companionship outside the confines of our family. Neither of them was the "love me forever" type.

Now you are probably wondering what it was like to

be a Jewish girl and then young woman growing up

as Nazism became the law of the land. Frankly, the

growth was so gradual, we hardly noticed. Grade

school years turned into high school without much of

the tension registering on my consciousness that was

just too full with being a teenager. I do remember

that as laws became more restrictive, we were not

allowed to participate in many aspects of school life.

This had unfortunate results for my school, since one

of my closest friends was our best gymnast. Once

she was banned from competition for being Jewish,

we never won any more prizes. And I do remember

my first encounter with Hitler Youth when we were

on vacation in 1933. There was a parade of the

young members—like a bunch of Cub Scouts in

America at a Fourth of July celebration—with bands

and flags and music, and my only memory is how much fun it looked like to march with all the others in their nice uniforms with their arms upraised in their proud salute. It wasn't about politics or racial hatred, but just about wanting to belong, which I suppose, is why those Hitler Youth participated so joyfully, too.

Then in 1935 things changed in a rush. The Nuremberg Laws were enacted, and I was no longer allowed to attend my old school with "good" Germans. So it was off to a Jewish private school, which—truth be told—was better than my old school, but I missed the friends I was forced to leave behind.

Life for me changed again the next year when the whole family moved back to Vienna.

Now she can finally fit into a dress from her
wardrobe. She starts putting it on. It is a girl's
evening gown. The DRESSER helps her into it.

I will never know what prompted my parents to

make this decision rather than emigrate from Europe

entirely. Hitler was casting a shadow over the whole

continent, but I think my Mother feared too severe a

change in her lifestyle and just wanted to go back

home. So instead of emigrating overseas, anywhere

overseas, my parents invested good money to move

to Vienna and renovate my grandmother's

apartment.

I settled once again into a new school and a new

routine. What stands out most in my memories of

1937 were the student dances. Every gymnasium

and many student organizations would give balls.

(SUSAN now has the dress on.) My first evening

gowns were made by the house seamstress—I told you it was a different world I lived in then. She would come for a day or two with patterns and her sewing machine. Even though I was only 15, I would never wear ready-made clothes. We all had seamstresses—even Father had his tailor—and Mother had her own modiste—a hat-maker. Thus in my world even hats were made to order. *(The DRESSER brings her a small bespoke hat and fits it lovingly onto her head.)*

Even dressed with such elegance, my teenage years were rather tame. Although I do remember 1937: my first date and the highlight of that first date—my first French kiss. The boy was close to 19. His name was Benno Gerstenhaber. I wonder if he made it through the carnage soon to descend on all of us.

*As SUSAN describes the following, The
DRESSER comes over and removes the party
dress ruthlessly. She gives SUSAN a cheap
coat to wear as she departs for the rest of her
life. The DRESSER's attitude toward SUSAN
becomes noticeably rougher.*

And descend it did in 1938. In March the Anschluss

changed our lives. Hitler annexed Austria—absorbed

it wholesale into Germany. Did we valiantly resist, as

the Poles would do fruitlessly the next year? No,

that was not the Austrian way. When the German

Army marched through our streets, they were

drowned in seas of flowers. And not only did our

neighbors receive the Nazis with great joy and

enthusiasm, they also went to work on anti-Semitic

excesses with a fervor I had not seen in Berlin at the

heart of the Reich. The gleeful anti-Semitism

displayed by the population was manifest in the

streets by making Jews do demeaning things, such as

clean the sidewalks or scrub out public toilets with toothbrushes. Anyone who even looked Jewish and sported a beard was stopped in the streets and had his beard cut off or even ripped out on the spot. But we didn't see such acts of humiliation in my neighborhood. The upper-class Austrians around us found such behavior beneath them. They were probably just as anti-Semitic, but they got their pound of flesh in a different way: they acquired all the property of the Jews almost as soon as it was confiscated by the Nazis.

> *The dress should be off by here. The DRESSER starts to put the removed dress on the rack, thinks better of it, and keeps it for herself.*

My father was in Prague when the armies invaded Vienna, and our Jewish friends began to flood out of Austria to supposed safety anywhere they could get that was not yet German occupied. And still, my

mother and I stayed. I think she did not want to

leave her jewelry and her beautiful apartment

behind. But the Gestapo came anyway and took

both. *(The DRESSER has now given her the coat.)* So

we were forced to flee with everyone else. Mother

and I flew to Prague to be with Father. The remnants

of our lives we were allowed to take with us: two

little suitcases.

> *The DRESSER takes two small suitcases and places them beside SUSAN, who picks them up and stands alone facing a very uncertain future as the lights fade. When they come back up, she is in a new place on stage.*

The future that greeted me was not much different

at first. *(SUSAN puts the suitcases down.)* But not

for long. Czechoslovakia soon fell under the same

shadow as Austria.   Our *new* home was absorbed

into the Reich.

> *The DRESSER takes the two suitcases,*
> *ransacks them, and tosses a cheap fur to*
> *SUSAN, who puts it on. The DRESSER then*
> *puts on a dress she takes from the other*
> *suitcase.*

We had arrived with little of our earlier lives and now

the Nazis quickly took most of what was left as they

confiscated as much Jewish wealth as they could—

jewelry, furs, electrical appliances—anything that

might help fund the war effort. When it was over,

we were able to keep a small radio and I still had a

little fur bolero. We next sought to escape to

Poland, which required crossing the border illegally.

Instead of leaving as a whole family, Mother insisted

that Father pave the way. She said

DRESSER:

(Now as Mother.) You go, and if you succeed in

crossing the border, the child and I will follow.

SUSAN:

That decision eventually cost her her life and me two

years in Birkenau.

> *At this thought SUSAN appears weakened by*
> *the memory. She removes the traveling coat*
> *and finally sits in the chair center stage. After*
> *a moment, she resumes the story.*

So father left alone—on August 31, 1939, and as they

say, the rest is history . The next day the German

war machine invaded Poland and World War II

began. Father must have managed to escape Poland

on one of the last planes leaving before every border

shut down.

In Prague the story was different: there was no last minute, dramatic flight for Mother and me.

DRESSER:

We are trapped. The Nazis have frozen our bank accounts. There is little for us to live on.

SUSAN:

(Again focusing on the audience as she shifts back to narration.) When the Blitzkrieg rolled over the Polish army in days, all countries of central Europe—Germany, Austria, Czechoslovakia, Poland—were now the German Third Reich. Mother and I were no longer foreign "guests" in Prague.

The DRESSER and SUSAN stare at each other across the void.

DRESSER:

We are homeless?

SUSAN:

We are nothing.

Now SUSAN turns from Mother and focuses briefly on the audience.

But there were still chances to get out.

SUSAN again appeals to Mother.

They are letting Jews emigrate to Palestine. We have

a real chance at that.

DRESSER:

(After a long moment, seeming to consider it.) No.

Get that silly notion out of your head.

During this section SUSAN often glares at Mother. There clearly is a tension between them.

SUSAN *(Focusing again on the audience):*

My other opportunity was to join my father, who had now fled to Belgium. If I had been allowed to go there, I could have then gone to America, as many of my cousins did. My father made numerous calls to Mother trying to get her to let me leave, even if she would not. Again, Mother would not permit it. She even kept the possibility of life in America from me. I only learned of this years later, after Mother had died in the camps and I had had to endure their horrors for two years—both of us victims of her decision to stay. Perhaps now you can understand why I am not particularly sentimental about my dear mother.

*The DRESSER as Mother exits, leaving SUSAN
alone to fend for herself.*

Since I knew nothing of this missed opportunity, I

lived a young woman's happy life in Prague.

> *At this thought, she gets up and goes to the
> rack herself, rummaging through the
> garments until she finds the party dress she
> wants and puts it on.*

I went to nightclubs, stayed out past the 8:00 pm

curfew—truly foolish, since being caught would

mean a quick ticket to a concentration camp—and I

had sex for the first time.

> *She stops her dressing to look directly at the
> audience, as if for their forgiveness or, at
> least, understanding. She then goes back to
> dressing and explains herself.*

I was in love—with a painter, Pips Schlesinger. And I

was rebelling against my mother, who I knew was

carrying on an affair of her own. Despite the times and with death and destruction surrounding us, we grabbed as much of life as we could. That manifested itself in promiscuity. I needed to be needed and loved by someone, anyone. Like the other young people around me, I mistook sexual fulfillment for that need. We dared, we pushed the envelope, we laughed, danced, and sang in the face of death. We would all live forever despite all the evidence around us saying that was not the case.

When she finishes the costume change, she twirls slowly, modeling her look for the audience and then sits in the chair again.

Life fell into a routine—again. I took courses such as gymnastics and later cosmetology, while I also had to work in a warehouse where we sorted out the goods stolen from families that had been deported East.

We sorted and the Nazis came and furnished their

homes in ways seldom seen in military quarters. In

October the transports began in earnest from Prague

to Litzmannsstadt. When families were sent East,

they were marched during the early morning hours

across the city and put on old passenger cars. This

occurred as the work day was starting. Anyone who

later claimed they knew nothing of the wholesale

transportation was a goddam liar. People stood and

stared silently. Some grinned, some cried, some

looked disturbed, but they all saw. They *all* saw.

And soon rumors came back about the horrible living

conditions in the Litzmannsstadt Ghetto: disease,

starvation, and death were daily occurrences. The

Nazis wanted to prevent any more details about

these very real conditions of the Jews being

revealed. So they devised the concept of a Prima

Ghetto—a showcase front to mask the atrocities already spreading in other ghettos and camps. Thus in November, 1941, was born Theresienstadt, which was quickly created to receive its "guests" as soon as possible.

Transports bound there began in January, 1942. That April we received our dreaded notice for transport. But that notice was done most "humanely." We weren't arrested. *(The DRESSER reenters still as Mother, reading a note and then handing it to SUSAN.)* Instead we received a very polite card telling us we would go on transport on May 7 and noting:

DRESSER *(Reading the "invitation"):*

We may take 50 kilograms of luggage, as well as

bedrolls for each of us and enough food for two days

of travel.

SUSAN:

It had all the appearance of an invitation.

DRESSER:

(With rising realization of their predicament.) An

invitation we cannot refuse.

SUSAN:

We were not to be prisoners—we were in what the

Nazis cynically referred to as "protective custody."

Protective custody. We needed protection from

them.

She tests the words on her tongue and makes it clear to her listeners that it is just so much bullshit.

The DRESSER goes through items on the rack and hands her the traveling coat again, which SUSAN puts on over her pitiful party dress. She then gives her one of the suitcases she had given her earlier. The DRESSER also dons a traveling coat and picks up her own valise.

The DRESSER goes through items on the rack and hands her the traveling coat again, which SUSAN puts on over her pitiful party dress. She then gives her one of the suitcases she had given her earlier. The DRESSER also dons a traveling coat and picks up her own valise.

Mother and I arrived at Theresienstadt on May 9, 1942. Soon afterward, selection began. Some were allowed to stay, while others were selected to "go East" to Poland—

DRESSER:

(As Mother.) To Sobibor, Maidanek, Chelmno, Treblinka, and Belzek.

SUSAN:

...all of which, we later learned, were places of no return—the extermination camps. Luck was with Mother and me. Because we knew one of the selectors, we were immediately told we were staying. *(SUSAN looks at the DRESSER, as Mother.)* But then Mother spoke up, asking for another favor.

DRESSER:

Can my good friend Rudi...

SUSAN:

(Over her to audience.) Lover.

DRESSER *(As Mother):*

...also stay? He is like a father to my girl.

SUSAN:

Since he was not really part of the family, that request was denied and he was to be transported East immediately.

DRESSER:

Then we don't stay either.

SUSAN:

(Glaring in disbelief at Mother, speaking directly to her.) No. I am staying. If you want to, you can stay with me, but I am staying.

DRESSER:

You are my daughter. You must go with us.

SUSAN:

(Now she speaks to the audience again.) Mother

was absolutely beside herself, but her love for Rudi

was stronger than her love and concern for me.

(Speaking to Mother again.) We shall meet

soon...for Christmas.

DRESSER:

(Echoing what they both know is a lie.) For

Christmas.

SUSAN:

(Speaking to the audience again, after a long look at

Mother.) These were the last words we ever spoke.

She then boarded the train that took her and Rudi to

the gas chambers of Sobibor. As the train pulled

away, she was shaking her head out of the window.

Did she know?

> *The DRESSER removes her Mother coat,*
> *dropping it to the floor. She shakes her head*
> *as described above and then retreats into the*
> *shadows. SUSAN is again alone.*

For the first time, I was really alone. After that I

seem to have largely a block about my memories of

Theresienstadt, and I don't know why. Possibly the

hell to come blotted out my memory. Certainly

there were plenty of deprivations, even in this

showcase ghetto: hunger, dirt, disease. Was it guilt

over my Mother: did I sense that her being sent East

was to be her death sentence? For whatever reason,

I have repressed this chapter in my Hegira to Hell.

> *She moves back to the rack, removing the*
> *traveling coat, picking up Mother's discarded*
> *coat along the way, and selecting a skirt.*
> *Instead of putting it on at this point, she holds*

it up against herself as she turns back to the audience.

I again turned to promiscuity. I had my first fling in the corner of a colonnade with a boy whose name, for the life of me, I can't remember.

But I do remember I was able to hold onto the dark-red plaid blanket from my luggage. I used it to make a fashionable bias-cut skirt. We women did not stop wanting new clothes just because it seemed to be impossible to get them.

This is the item she has held up against herself. She puts it on.

And we procured other things as well. I even got hold of a stolen pot-bellied stove. Life was as good as it would be for a long time to come. And I fell in love—fully and permanently in love—with a young doctor in the ghetto. His name was Ernstl. *(The DRESSER enters, assuming the persona of the lover. As it is described, they stroll hand in hand and then dance to the background music.)* My promiscuous relationships ended as I gave all my love and myself to him. We walked the grounds as if lovers in a park, attended the clandestine cabarets and music performances of American-style jazz, *(A Benny Goodman tune has come up in the background)* and shared food cooked on that stolen stove.

But it was that stove that proved my downfall. The person who had stolen it for us turned us in, and I was immediately slated to be sent East to Birkenau as a thief. *(She clings onto her lover.)*

Saying goodbye to Ernstl was the worst feeling I had ever experienced. Since I had no idea what awaited me at the end of my eastern journey, I was more heartbroken about separation from the great love of my life. *(They separate reluctantly and The DRESSER fades into the shadows.)* I saw him for a fleeting moment at Birkenau. I never learned his fate. I'd like to think he survived and made a good life for himself—but that is just fantasy.

This is the reality: I was sent East on an antiquated passenger car, which I knew was better than the cattle cars that were typically used to move us human cattle to our doom. At least this car had a bathroom—a filthy, stinking toilet—but a vast improvement over a bucket to piss and shit in. We almost lost track of the days, but from the rising and setting of the sun I could tell we were moving East. The train wasn't heated, but I don't remember the January cold. There must have been enough tightly-packed body heat to keep us fairly warm. Then on

January 31, 1943—or it may have been February 1—

not important. That marked my arrival in hell.

Whatever preceded in my life was the first chapter in

my story. The second one, the creation of a new

person, the trial by fire literally, started now.

> *She stands alone, this time with nothing but*
> *the clothes on her back. There is a distinct*
> *change in the lighting, with levels rising to an*
> *almost painful intensity.*

On that night we pulled up to a brightly lit platform.

We must have passed through the now-infamous

towered archway leading into the Birkenau

compound at Auschwitz, but I didn't see it from my

tightly-wedged position on a bench in the train car.

When the train stopped, the doors were flung open.

We were immediately hit by a repulsive stink

emanating from a smokestack, its flames topped by

swirling black clouds of smoke.

*The DRESSER shouts "Raus, raus" and SUSAN
is thrown down on the stage and is
immediately bathed in an intense light.*

I looked up and saw a wide railroad platform

bordered by long barbed-wire fences—so long I

couldn't see the beginning or the end. Wooden

guard towers with machine guns aimed at regular

intervals along the fences. There were bright lights

everywhere—on the towers, on the fences. Facing

us stood a field-gray ambulance with Red Cross

logos. That symbol of help and safety gave us a

modicum of hope. It worked as the Nazis intended

—it kept the sheep quiet. If we only knew then its

true purpose—to carry tins of Cyclon B gas to the

"showers" and bring the empty tins back to be

refilled for the next harvest of Jews.

We women were then lined up in rows of five next to the train. *(SUSAN stands and comes to as close a simulation of "attention" as she can muster.)* We never saw the men after leaving the passenger car. But we did see men in SS gray and others in what seemed to be gray-and-blue striped pants and jackets. They wore brimless round caps on their bald heads. Surprisingly, they looked neither dirty nor emaciated. These were men from the *Kanada* commando, the work detail in charge of the prisoners' possessions—the elite detail of the Birkenau compound.

Once we were lined up a medical officer separated us. Girls under 14 or 15 and women over 35-40, as well as all mothers with their children were loaded onto trucks. *(She moves to the side, as if pushed that direction, while looking at the other unseen group.)* I

remember thinking, how lucky they were to ride.
The filled trucks then headed toward the
smokestacks. Just like the men, we never saw them
again either.

We few remnants of the so-called transported
"pieces"—about 60 out of the 500 females who
arrived alive on the train—were marched through a
gate in the fence and herded into a pre-fab barrack
with a dirt floor and a few dim lights—nothing more.
*(SUSAN moves to another part of the stage, where
she is greeted by The DRESSER, dressed as described
below. The lights are much dimmer here.)* Shaved-
headed female prisoners in civilian clothing with a
broad red stripe down the back moved among us
taking any jewelry and valuables that had not already
been stolen from us.

The DRESSER indicates for SUSAN to sit and then roughly takes a locket from her.

We then settled in for the night on the cold floor.

(SUSAN sinks down to the floor.) The night guards

all-too-eagerly answered our wary questions.

DRESSER*:*

(Stooping down and whispering.) You are the lucky

ones. The trucks took the others to the gas.

SUSAN:

They gave us detailed horror stories of the gas

chamber disguised as a shower and the

crematorium. We could only stare back in disbelief.

(The DRESSER stands and smirks or even laughs, then

exits.) The questions stopped. I was strangely

detached from the incredibility of what I had heard.

*The lights slowly fade to black on SUSAN
sitting alone on the stage.*

*As the lights fade back up, SUSAN is standing
up. The DRESSER, as an SS officer, stands
behind her.*

In the morning we were led to be processed-in at the

Sauna—a room with actual heating and showers.

But first, we were thrust into a large anteroom

guarded by SS men.

DRESSER:

(As an SS man.) Strip. Everything off. Everything.

SUSAN:

I felt like I was standing outside myself, calmly taking

off all my clothes. *(She does so slowly into a*

suggestion of nudity—body stocking, leotard or the

like.) We were then shorn from top to bottom of all

body hair.

> *The DRESSER puts a flesh-colored stocking cap on SUSAN to indicate her baldness. The DRESSER then moves up toward the costume rack, pulling several items off the rack.*

It was supposed to be for hygiene—after all the bugs

loved naked flesh even more—but in reality was one

of the seemingly countless processes calculated to

dehumanize us. They wanted us shorn, not just of

our hair, but of dignity, self-esteem and the sense of

self-preservation.

We were next chased into a shower room and given

an ice-cold shower and left to dry in the winter air.

We were handed our clothing next:

> *The DRESSER dumps the clothes unceremoniously at SUSAN's feet and then watches as she dresses.*

blue and white striped shifts, boxer shorts with tie

strings. Then we were given khaki colored long pants

and jackets buttoned to the neck. The coats were

adorned with blood and bullet holes, since they were

actually Russian uniforms from captured and gassed

POWs. If we were lucky, we got ill-fitting,

mismatched shoes. If unlucky, we got clogs that

chafed with all the running we had to do—never any

slow-walking for us—and often led to gangrene.

Next came tattooing on the left forearm. *(The*

DRESSER grabs her arm and does this rather

hurriedly.) We got a five digit number with an

upside-down triangle underneath. Mine was 34042.

The triangle identified us as Jewish women from

transport and thus eligible for gassing. The men got

only a number. They needed no triangle to identify

them as Jews. Circumcision marked them all too

clearly.

> *When she finishes with the tattooing, The*
> *DRESSER hands SUSAN a kerchief.*

Then we were given a kerchief to cover our bald

heads and to serve as our only towel or napkin. They

had to be tied just so. *(She ties her kerchief*

properly.) If you failed to tie yours properly, you

were often singled out as too weak and then sent to

the gas. Next we were given a strip of cloth with our

number on it.

DRESSER:

(Attaching the number to the clothing.) Left side

over the breast of the uniform.

> *The DRESSER attaches the number to the*
> *clothing.*

Now properly clothed, we were given our only possession—a brick-red metal bowl ten inches wide and five inches deep. *(The DRESSER gets it from upstage and hands it to SUSAN.)* We had no spoon, no knife, no fork, no cup, no saucer, no plate. Nor did we have toothbrush, handkerchief, towel, nor comb. You had nothing. You were at the level of an animal.

Next we were moved along to the new-arrival blocks, which the Nazis sardonically called the "quarantine" block. It was a stone building that looked like a large chicken house. It housed 800 women on two-tiered bunks with five or six women per bunk. The floors were dirt. There were no washing facilities, no toilets. Outside the block, one latrine and one pitiful water faucet were shared by each row of three such buildings. The *stubovas*—the cleaning and maintenance prisoners, who had survived months in the camp already—could be quite ruthless with the newcomers and pushed us into the block and screamed at us to

DRESSER:

Find a *Koje*.

SUSAN:

The name for the bunks. One of the *stubovas* told me:

DRESSER:

Get a place on a top bunk. If you're smart.

SUSAN:

It was my first lesson in survival. I soon learned the reason. When the nighttime slop buckets overflowed with urine and feces, we prisoners were forced to relieve ourselves in the only way we could—into our red bowls. The only way then to empty it out was to pour our waste down the wall beside the bunk. If you were located below...

(After a long pause to let it sink in.) The filth—from not having water to wash properly, from soiling ourselves when not reaching our moment at the latrines in time—was part of the planned dehumanizing process. As a result, fleas, lice, bedbugs became our companions almost immediately. After a latrine visit we got our only drinkable liquid—a black mixture the guards called coffee. We filled our bowls with it. Then came our

second lesson: if we had used our bowls to relieve

ourselves during the night, we had better have

already washed them out from the faucet near the

latrine. We quickly learned lesson three—to wash

hands and face with that same black liquid, since we

had no other water source. We knew a dirty face or

hands singled us out and led to the gas.

       There is a shrill whistle and SUSAN quickly
       stands as if in line.

DRESSER:

Zahlappell! Quickly in line. Rollcall.

SUSAN:

To determine the daily body count: how many alive,

how many dead, how many diseased, how many

detached on special work assignments. We packed

ourselves together as tightly as we could for warmth.

The count occurred day after day, come rain or shine or snow or heat or freezing temperature. We stood and stood. If someone gave up, hanging back in the barrack or simply lying down in line to die, we had to start the count again, since we couldn't come up one dirty Jewess short.

After the hours-long count came the *Aussenkommando Kapos* selecting prisoners for their respective work details. We quickly learned which *Kapo* to avoid and which to seek—who would quickly work us literally to death and who might just let us survive.

It was on that first day of work that I began to claw my way toward surviving: I stepped out of line and went up to an SS man. *(SUSAN approaches The DRESSER.)* *"Melde gehorsamst ich bin ein Bureaukraft."* I don't know if this was out of bravery, ignorance of the rules, or sheer stupidity, but it worked.

DRESSER:

An office worker? *(A smile or even a short laugh. Then pulling SUSAN's arm and writing down her number as she walks away.)*

SUSAN:

He would remember me after that.

(She is again alone on stage.) Our food was minimal. We were served a liquified mess they called "soup." It sometimes had weeds or pieces of potato peel floating in it. It made me gag that first time, but soon hunger made me eagerly gulp it down. Another lesson: eat anything that looked edible, even weeds

or cigarette butts; we ate them all to keep away

hunger.

Work fell into a routine. Morning rollcall, marching

to hard labor, return at the end of the day, another

inspection and selection for the gas. After dark the

trucks would pull up and load the daily harvest of

death. They all knew where they were going.

Despite their weakness and broken spirits, they did

not go quietly. I remember those trucks most vividly

on Christmas eve 1943. One of the SS had decided

we Jews needed a little celebration of Jesus so we

were allowed to cut a little tree and decorate with

chains made of colored paper. While we sang

Christmas carols accompanied by the camp

orchestra, a convoy of trucks doing the daily drive to

death passed by. Neither our singing nor the

orchestra was loud enough to drown out the cries,

prayers, and curses of those doomed women. Thus did the Third Reich celebrate the holiest day in Christendom.

Soon, however, my brash approach to the SS officer about my skills paid off. I was told not to march out one morning. Instead I went to the Sauna, where I was told to clothe myself in a gray and blue camp dress with a three-quarter jacket. *(SUSAN begins to change with the assistance of The DRESSER.)* The clothes were hard and rough. Then I was marched to Auschwitz I—the main camp, the KZ, the concentration camp, to distinguish it from Birkenau, the death camp—through a gate with the legend written above it: *"Arbeit macht frei*—Work makes you free."* We were never to be free.

I was led to a barracks housing the so-called Political Department but actually the Gestapo headquarters.

I was given my "job interview" by sitting me in front

of a typewriter and being told to type the transcript

of an interrogation conducted in front of me. I

remember typing furiously all day being dictated to

by the SS officer what he wanted on the record. I

tried to tune out the cries of the nameless prisoner

who was being beaten mercilessly. I apparently

passed the test. About a week later, I was given

fresh clothes, better fitting shoes, and got my head

freshly shaved. *(Her shoes are replaced with a better*

matching pair.) I was now suitable in appearance to

be a full-fledged member of the work detail for the

offices of the Gestapo. There were definite

advantages. I was assigned to one of the dormitories

in the basement with clean bathrooms, bed linens,

and heated rooms.

We did all the administrative work for the entire Auschwitz complex, working either as private secretaries to the leading SS men or in the so-called *Standesamt* or bridal registry office—another cynical SS joke. I was assigned to a twenty-girl secretarial pool that recorded the daily deaths in the camps—the aforementioned "bridal registry." We remained incredibly busy every day.

Unfortunately this almost-haven away from the death camp didn't last long for me. Someone broke the rules and the newest recruits were punished collectively. I was to return to Birkenau and would now experience its true unending horror.

> *The DRESSER brings in her old clothes, dumping them at SUSAN's feet. She waits as the nicer clothes are taken off and returned to her.*

Despite the short time of my stay away, return to

Birkenau was again traumatic. *(The memory is*

difficult for SUSAN, who sits again in the chair for this

part of her story.) I found myself in a different block,

so the first thing I needed was to find a new group to

offer me collective support. Women nurtured one

another. It was better to survive collectively rather

than to give up and die alone. I got into a group of

older women 35-40 years old—truly old for survivors

in the death camp. This was fortunate because I

soon became deathly ill with typhus fever after a day

of standing naked in the cold for de-lousing. The

members of my group gave me more food to help

keep up my strength. When I could barely stand at

roll call each morning, two of them held me up. In

the field they kept me as sheltered as possible from

doing any real physical labor. Despite all this help,

the *blockova,* who had befriended me only because I could speak Czech with her, warned me:

DRESSER:

Susie, tomorrow you must go to Block 27.

SUSAN:

That was the "hospital" block—a euphemism for the death block, the ante-chamber to the gas and the crematorium. *(Now addressing The DRESSER.)* Give me one more day of rest in our block. One more day to get better.

> *There is a long pause. The DRESSER gives an almost imperceptible nod, places something in SUSAN'S hand, and then exits.*

She gave me one Vitamin C tablet and one aspirin and one more day. *(Long pause.)* Strange to say, the miracle did happen. The fever broke that night.

Vitamin C? Aspirin? Luck? *(Another pause while she ponders her fate.)* I avoided the attention of the SS, escaped the trip to the gas, and got stronger day by day. Without those other women, without that small act of kindness from the *blockova*—if that's what it was—I would have been doomed.

Soon after that my good luck held—all things are relative, aren't they? I was transferred to an elite detail, which meant I had to leave the group that had saved my life. It was difficult letting go, but it taught me another hard lesson: do not get too attached to anyone.

> *This time she almost joyously throws off the work detail clothes to don her new administrative clothes.*

July 1943. I emerged from possibly my worst time in the camp to my best the *Schreibstube*—the

Administrative Office. My first stop was the Sauna again, where I got a real shower, a fresh shaving of the head, lotion to kill the bedbugs and lice, and even new camp underwear. I was delighted in the blue and white stripe dress, black apron, and white kerchief I was given. And then—miracle of miracles—new shoes and even stockings.

Suitably, almost fashionably clothed, I received the assignment to sit on a high stool recording women prisoners' names in a big book. *(She sits in the chair and demonstrates the job.)* Whenever someone died, I drew a line through the entry in the book. As camp jobs went, this was about as good as they got. But it was short-lived when I was falsely accused of stealing bread. *(The DRESSER removes the chair, pushing it upstage.)* Transfer to another detail, but at least I remained indoors for my work duty. I was assigned to the *Bauleitung* or construction detail.

My job there was to type plans for future camps like Auschwitz spreading all the way across Eastern Europe and Russia to the Ural Mountains. But typical of the Nazis, they had to keep us down somehow, so our job also included serving as cleaning women, scrubbing floors on our hands and knees. *(SUSAN is on the floor scrubbing when The DRESSER enters, dressed as a male prisoner.)*

DRESSER:

(Beckoning to SUSAN.) Up. *(SUSAN looks up, but otherwise does nothing.)* Off your knees, and follow me. I have something special for you. *(SUSAN still does not respond.)* Food.

SUSAN:

(She rises and then follows warily.) I was led to a storage room by this habitual criminal prisoner, who proceeded to rape me on the store room floor.

> *SUSAN's dress is torn off and tossed aside and she is knocked to the floor and The DRESSER retreats to the clothes rack after tossing something at SUSAN's feet.*

I was left with two things by the brute—a piece of sausage thrown at me for payment and a case of VD—a good dose of the clap. I was sent to the hospital ward and again nursed back to health by friends. Miraculously, I escaped the typical consequence of contracting such a disease, in fact any disease—a trip to the gas.

When I was released from the ward, I needed to be reassigned for work. *(SUSAN rises from the floor and*

The DRESSER helps her into new, better clothes than ever before in the camp.) This time to *Kanada*, the best work detail in Birkenau, so-called because it was the land of everything—food, clothing, medicine, virtually anything that came on the transports. We had access to anything we could smuggle in, so long as we did not get caught.

One of the joys of my new good fortune was new underwear. Gone were the boxers. I now had silk and cotton panties, as well as a virtual miracle—a bra for the first time since entering the camp. Also an overabundance of handkerchiefs, nightgowns, nail files, knives, spoons and sheets for my straw bed. All were taken from the new arrivals.

I was assigned to the night shift. *(The DRESSER slides the chair back into place and SUSAN sits.)* We stayed busy because the arrivals began to accelerate.

Knowing they had lost the war, the Nazis were determined not to lose the Final Solution. So we now received daily arrivals from the East as well as the West, as the Nazis tried to rid the world of as many Jews as they could before the fall of the Third Reich.

Yes, we had access to virtually anything, but we could not afford to think about where the things we sorted and bundled for shipment came from. We couldn't afford to put a face to that woman's skirt or that man's suit or that child's dress. We could only think about our continued survival. We "old" prisoners had clawed our way up to that work detail through knowing someone who knew someone or by being at the right place at the right time. We were people who had lost touch with the normal values of the world outside. We lived for ourselves, for our

friends, for our group.

Sometimes we would be brought back to reality,

would regain some of our humanity. While I was

working on the sorting heaps, *(The DRESSER hands*

her a photograph.) I came across a photo of two

young people obviously very much in love. I took a

closer look, because something seemed familiar

about them. I knew these two from my days in

Prague a year before the deportations began. I

stood for a minute with the photo in my hand. There

was no real chance either of them was still alive. I

did not keep the photo. *(SUSAN drops the picture to*

the floor.) What for?

I had doubts about the existence of a God. How

could anyone think of a loving God who watches

over every one of us, when that God would have

looked down on Birkenau and its smoking chimneys?

How could anyone, even the most fanatically

religious believer, contemplate that the kind of

suffering delivered to us could have anything to do

with the will of an almighty God? That in itself would

be almost blasphemous. I laughed at any prisoners

who claimed that the suffering we were enduring

strengthened their faith. Hypocrisy. Whose side was

God on? The Jew, the Muslim, the Christian, the

Nazi? I could no longer believe in a god that so far

had saved me but let millions of others die. What

did they die for? Their faith? No, they died due to

hatred and fanatic bigotry and greed.

> *The lights fade to black momentarily. Then*
> *when they come back up, we see SUSAN*
> *sitting on the floor, sorting.*

The work continued. This routine was seldom

interrupted by anything dramatic—just sorting,

recording, and surviving one day more. And then the

Russians came. Not in tanks or jeeps, not in ranks of

soldiers marching into the camp to free us, but

through the air.

> *SUSAN walks downstage looking up to the*
> *sky. A sound of planes in large formation is*
> *heard followed by alarms.*

As soon as the alarm sounded, the SS men

disappeared. The *Kanada* compound was deserted

by all but us prisoners. We stood gazing up at the

sky with wonder. With each bomb we heard

exploding, we cheered. I was standing at a window,

screaming to the skies. *(She sings joyously.)* "We're

hanging our washing on the Siegfried line, if the

Siegfried line's still there." *(The DRESSER then joins*

her for another verse.) While we later heard some

prisoners were killed by the bombs in other parts of

the camp, we prayed for more. It was a tremendous

high, and for the first time we felt there might be

life—and not just the crematorium--waiting for us.

That sense of hope only strengthened when we

learned in June, 1944, that the Allies had landed on

European soil in France—D-Day. Despite this

growing sense of hope's return, I was not fully

convinced that freedom was near.

> *The lights again fade on this dark moment. In*
> *the dark another brief raid can be heard. As it*
> *fades, the lights come back up on SUSAN, who*
> *is again seated in the chair.*

The air raids were few—too few to our liking and

never took out the crematoriums. We supposed the

Allies were fearful of killing us prisoners, but our lives

were forfeit anyway. Maybe it had a simpler

explanation: it's just Jews. Why bother?

As 1944 drew to a close, we heard more rumors that

the war was faring badly for the Germans. Such

news emboldened the prisoners to the point that

they revolted in Cremo IV. There were retributions,

but the gassing finally stopped for good on

November 2. Order continued to break down as

rules were relaxed to the point that one jazz-loving

SS man learned of my love of that music. One

afternoon, he led me and a male prisoner to an out

of the way spot, where we spent a joyous few hours

singing—surprisingly to the SS-man's

accompaniment of us on the accordion, which he

played very well.

There is a brief interlude as we hear a jazz
tune, such as "Stardust," with a background

accordion. SUSAN sings the song until the memory fades.

It was like a moment out of time, three young people making music without any regard to the deep gulf that separated us. The SS seemed to have lost their zeal for their mission.

Then on the night of January 17-18, 1945, my hell on earth at Auschwitz ended: the entire complex was shut down, and we were evacuated into the Reich and away from the rapidly advancing Russian Red Army. We were roused in the barracks.

DRESSER:

(As *SS man.*) Go to the warehouse and find warm clothing. Take knapsacks and stuff them with socks, underwear—anything to keep you warm. We are going on a long walk.

SUSAN:

Those orders saved 500 lives.

DRESSER:

A bullet in the head for those who cannot walk.

The DRESSER throws down a knapsack at SUSAN's feet.

SUSAN:

And so the "Death March" began. *(SUSAN runs up to the clothes rack and franticly loads the knapsack, puts on a heavy coat and starts to walk in a circle around the stage.)* For two days and nights we walked through forests covered in snow, the roads lined with bodies. Many fled—went "over the hill"— when the opportunity presented itself. But my group from the *Kanada* block stayed with the

march—15 of us prodded along by three SS men.
Eventually we reached a railroad where we were
herded into an open coal car and moved deeper into
the Reich toward our unknown fate. We came to a
big city. My open-air view let me see the bombed
out, dilapidated buildings, block after block of them.
I gloried in the ruin of a city I had once loved. It was
Berlin.

We passed on through and arrived at a huge
women's concentration camp—Ravensbruck.

SUSAN stops her walking.

Our SS guards from Birkenau stayed with us and kept
the group together. They managed to get us
assigned to a warehousing situation, given our well-
developed expertise from *Kanada* detail. We got
better barracks, better clothes, better food. We

even received Red Cross humanitarian packages.

They had been coming for years, but had never

trickled down to our level at Birkenau. These

packages even contained cigarettes. *(She lights one*

and glories in it. Then she has a thought.) You don't

think they knew these things cause cancer, do you?

(She stubs it out and rises from the chair to continue

the story.) Then we learned :

DRESSER:

The Russians are nearby .

SUSAN:

They are headed to liberate us.

DRESSER:

They are coming to rape you.

Taking this in, SUSAN shifts her focus back to the audience.

SUSAN:

We were roused by the Nazis to march away from

the "liberating" force. *(She starts to remove some of*

her heavier winter clothing.) They kept us moving at

a brisk pace by warning us:

DRESSER:

(Again stepping down.) Don't fall behind. The

Russians will get you.

SUSAN laughs at this, thinking about all she has already been put through by the Nazis, and then continues the story after The DRESSER retreats.

We marched all through the night. The goal was to

reach the American lines—safety for us—from the

Nazis, from the Russians—and a chance for our SS

guards to survive, something they knew would not

happen if they were overtaken by the avenging,

rampaging Red Army. Survival was primary. Sleep

was secondary.

Then on May 1, a motorcycle roared by us with the

rider shouting over and over:

DRESSER:

The *Fuhrer* is dead! The *Fuhrer* is dead!

SUSAN:

(Taking up the cry, both shouting together.) The

Fuhrer is dead! *The Fuhrer* is dead!

Within minutes the impromptu celebration began. I

shouted, "We're free now!" When the sense of

euphoria died down, we continued West along with

our SS guards. I suppose we felt safer with them

than without them. Then there was a commotion

ahead of us. A vehicle was making its way slowly

toward us. It had a large white star on the hood.

Everyone knew only one star symbol. We muttered:

DRESSER and SUSAN *(together)*:

Russians.

SUSAN:

After all our efforts we had been overtaken after all.

But then the vehicle stopped, and I saw written

below the windshield, "Daisy Mae." That didn't

seem Russian to me so I stepped forward and said in

my halting school-girl English, "Can you help us?"

The Yankee driver looked surprised.

DRESSER:

(Now assuming the American soldier persona.) You speak English.

SUSAN:

(Speaking slowly, choosing her words carefully.) We are prisoners from Birkenau. *(There is no recognition, response from the American.)* An ... *(searching for the right word.)* ... extermination camp.

DRESSER:

What the hell is an extermination camp?

> *SUSAN glares and then holds up her arm to reveal her number. There is an uncomfortable pause as the truth of what she has said registers with the soldier.*

DRESSER:

We are scouts. *(As with SUSAN before, the soldier seeks the right words to get her to understand.)* An advanced American unit.

> *SUSAN nods slowly to let the soldier know she understands.*

SUSAN:

(Pleading.) Will you let our guards know their Reich is finished?

DRESSER:

(Looking her in the eye.) You tell them for me.

> *SUSAN again lets the moment sink in. Again she nods and turns to the guards, but the soldier adds to his orders.*

DRESSER:

And tell them to give *you* their weapons.

SUSAN:

(After a pause she moves downstage to the unseen guards.) Hauptscharfuhrer, the American officer wants your gun. *(She reaches out her hands to receive the weapons.)* All three reluctantly gave me their guns.

> *She then goes to The DRESSER and mimes handing over a gun.*

Where should we go?

DRESSER:

(Without much thought.) Keep walking to the next town.

SUSAN:

(Not getting the answer she wanted to hear, she again moves on.) With that command, we obeyed as we had been taught to do by the Nazis.

> *SUSAN circles silently about the stage. Then she stops abruptly.*

SUSAN:

Eventually we saw an American checkpoint. We approached a group of soldiers sitting on and standing around a strange looking vehicle—a jeep—we later learned it was called. Again, I asked, "Where should we go?"

DRESSER:

(Representing another American.) You go back where you came from.

SUSAN:

I knew then it was time to stop following orders

slavishly, as we had been so carefully taught. I spoke

up. *(Now addressing the American soldier directly.)* I

don't think so. *(She again shows her prisoner*

number.) Number 34042. We were death camp

prisoners. Now we are survivors. So you tell me

again where we should go.

DRESSER:

(Pausing to think it over) I guess that leaves you to

us.

> *There is a long pause, as the realization sinks*
> *in. SUSAN then addresses the audience again.*

SUSAN:

My war was over.

Lights fade slowly to black. When they come back up, The DRESSER is helping SUSAN get ready for her final journey of the night.

SUSAN:

(As she is being dressed.) After changing locations as a "displaced person," I learned through an old friend of my parents that my father had survived the war— hiding in Brussels throughout the conflict. *(The DRESSER gives SUSAN one last look, adjusts something, and sends her on her way.)* In July, 1945, I received permission to enter Belgium and took the train to Brussels. With my schoolgirl French I managed to find the right trolley car and to get out at the right stop—Rue Turvueren—and found the right apartment house. I went up the stairs... *(She adjusts her clothes, puts away a slip of paper with*

*the address on it, straightens her hair.) ...*and rang

the bell.

> *She mimes pushing the doorbell and then*
> *stands expectantly, waiting as the lights fade*
> *to black. After a moment the lights come*
> *back up as SUSAN is being redressed by the*
> *DRESSER in the clothes SUSAN entered in.*

SUSAN:

It was an emotional reunion: He had not changed at

all. I think we both cried. It had been almost 6 years

since he had left Prague and since both of our lives

had taken frightful and miraculous turns that

ultimately kept us both alive. I settled in to live with

him—and his mistress, who was not much older than

I. Do I need to tell you that created an awkward

situation?

> *The DRESSER gives SUSAN one last look,*
> *adjusts something, and exits.*

If you take anything away from my musings tonight, let it be this: Truth does not exist on a situational continuum—big truths, little truths, small lies, big lies. No, there are only truths and lies. Despite what you may have heard, truth *is* truth.

I have heard it said that during the Holocaust God averted his face from mankind, and now he has returned to mankind. That I can accept and that I can deal with. And so I have a certain amount of my faith back. I am still skeptical, but I can enjoy a traditional reform service at synagogue. The familiar prayers relax me and give me a modicum of peace.

But for all the reassurance I get from such traditions, I get that faith tested when I look around me and see the threats lurking—and now it seems all too often emerging from the darkness into the bright light of day. When I hear hate spouted from political platforms, when I see people who should know

better enabling those forces by their complicity,

when I watch in disbelief as people march in the

streets of a quiet college town carrying torches and

displaying the same symbols that stole my youth and

most of my friends and family from me, when I see

families seeking political asylum only to have

children ripped from their mothers' arms, children

led away for clean clothes and showers never then to

return. When I see death visited on the faithful

worshiping their God in a Charleston church or a

Pittsburgh synagogue... I wonder just how safe we

are. Is God averting his head again?

> *The lights fade one final time.*

> *An image of SUSAN late in life comes up in the darkness as the actress playing SUSAN exits. Simultaneously The DRESSER enters from the other side of the stage. She is carrying the*

distinctive jacket that SUSAN is wearing in the image.

DRESSER:

Susan was actively involved in the evolution of this play and was able to attend a performance of the world premiere production. She left us on November 17, 2019, at age 97, exactly two weeks after seeing the play. This play is our thank you to her for a life that embodied the strength of the human spirit.

> *The DRESSER takes the jacket she is holding and hangs it on the rack. She exits. The image of SUSAN remains as the strains of "Stardust" are again heard. This time it is a recording of SUSAN singing the song in a rehearsal of the show. The image and the recording fade together. We are left in darkness.*

Susan Cernyak-Spatz

Memoirist

Susan Cernyak-Spatz was born in Vienna in 1922 and ran the gamut of the Holocaust ordeal from refugee in 1938 to internment in Theresienstadt in 1942, deportation to Auschwitz-Birkenau in 1943, the Death March in 1945, and liberation in May of 1945.

As Professor Emerita in German literature at UNC-Charlotte, she continued to teach as well as frequently lecture in the United States and in Europe on her experiences during the Holocaust.

She passed away in November, 2019, exactly two weeks after attending a performance of the world premiere of this play.

Charles LaBorde

Playwright

Charles LaBorde has been an actor, director, designer, and playwright, as well as an arts educator and administrator throughout his lifetime. He holds a Ph.D. from The Ohio State University in theatre and doctoral certification in educational administration from the University of North Carolina. He was the founder of the high school at Northwest School of the Arts in Charlotte, where he served as principal for 15 years until his retirement in 2008.

He has received 11 regional and state directing awards, a national directing award from the National Youth Theatre, and numerous awards for scenic, costume, lighting, and sound design from the North Carolina Theatre Conference (NCTC). As a playwright he has received two national and four regional playwriting awards and has had his play, *Memorial*, performed in New York, across the nation, and in Europe. That play remains in print more than twenty-five years after its initial publication.

His most recent plays are *Affinity*—about Frank Lloyd Wright and the murders at Taliesen—and *Unbound*—about the Wright Brothers at Kitty Hawk, North Carolina.

In 2010 he was named both Best Actor in a Drama and Theatre Person of the Year by Creative Loafing and was awarded the Marian Smith Lifetime Career Achievement Award by NCTC. He was also honored by having the black box theatre at Northwest School of the Arts renamed the Charles LaBorde Theatre.

He is a full member of The Dramatists Guild, Inc.—the professional theatre association of playwrights, composers, and lyricists.